A NEW LEAF

A NEW LEAF

Pip McCormac and Jennifer Haslam

Hardie Grant

BOOKS

Contents

Introduction

By Pip McCormac, co-author

All of the people you're about to meet, all the architects, the designers and creatives, have meticulously thought about every corner of their homes. Every angle has been finessed, every material painstakingly chosen, every colour and texture compared to others and finally alighted upon. And all of these people have also chosen to include plants, liberally and displayed as prized parts of the decor. What was fascinating to me, as we started off on this project, was why.

Plants and design have gone hand in hand for years. From the way Frank Lloyd Wright set iconic houses like Fallingwater amongst oak, red maple and hickory trees in 1935 to how Mies van der Rohe's Farnsworth House (completed in 1951) was essentially built to appreciate the beauty of the sugar maple tree in front of it, architects have long had a fascination with and been inspired by the natural world. More recently, succulents took over social media while fiddle leaf figs, monstera and Chinese money plants became part of the furniture – literally – in homes seen across the design pages of any and every magazine. How many of us have houseplants we treat as members of the family, or pets? Giving them names, taking care of them, watching as they evolve?

In the homes we have featured throughout these pages the foliage isn't a late addition, or an afterthought or a nod to an increasing trend. Their inclusion was built into the very fabric of the scheme, sometimes even chosen and thought about before any walls had been put up and windows put in. Intriguingly, in every single interview, each homeowner had an entirely different and unique reason for wanting to fill their home with fronds.

Some conversations talk about the way that plants round the hard edges of brutalist decor, and there are certainly plenty of concrete walls here that come alive when a sprawling ficus is placed in front of them. Others talk about how having plants in their space help them feel a connection to their home, perhaps by having a living part of their house that needs regular daily attention, or in the way the shadows their leaves cause on the walls at different points of the day during different times of the year helps them notice the passing of the seasons. Others mention that whereas architecture is a finite art – you build something and it's pretty much complete – plants keep changing and growing, while others, even those

who have created some of the world's most intriguing, unusual and exciting structures, talk about how the fascinating shape of the leaves on a plant fill them with daily wonder. I was struck by how reverential people were as they spoke about their plants, how many times I was told people simply couldn't live without them in their homes. How the plants provided more than just a nice hobby to take care of, and instead were innate to the way people lived.

'The homes all have a softness to them, thanks to the plants,' says Jennifer Haslam, my co-author and the art director of the shoots. 'They all just had life to them. In not one of the homes were the leaves completely pristine, or perfect, or felt placed. Instead, you could tell the plants were there because they were loved, giving personality and depth to these houses, none of which came across as remotely staged.'

The plants you'll see here are as varied as the reasons behind their inclusion. Some are tropical, some are giant, some have been grown from seed and others have been shipped in at full height. Ficus feature prominently, along with avocado trees, ferns and monsteras. Yet curiously, the most common theme that runs through is how infrequently the home owners knew the names of the plants they have. People who were able to reference the specific types of brick used in their properties often had no idea what their plants were called, implying a totally different relationship to the houses themselves and the natural elements they've chosen to include.

It makes sense, in a way. Many of these peoples' jobs revolve around precision, around creating projects for clients and for themselves that are controlled and contained down to the very smallest fraction. Embracing plant life is a way to factor in the unknown, something that is harder to control and will often bend to its own will. It creates a feeling of awe in a space over which the homeowners have totally exerted their command and authority, allowing for imagination to run as wild as the tendrils on a creeping vine. And while the aesthetics you'll see here differ, the sense of joy that comes from the plants stays constant throughout. The plants allow the home to grow with the homeowner, creating a notion of ever-changing delight around which they can see their design handiwork in a new light. Turning over a new leaf, if you will. A new thinking about what interiors mean.

Ben Richardson

Co-founder of Metro Imaging
Vauxhall, London, UK

THE GREENERY IN BEN RICHARDSON'S warehouse conversion in south London was chosen for its structural beauty, with the jutting arms of a towering cactus and the bowing branches of a giant rubber plant appearing like modern installations. Against the backdrop of smooth, polished-to-a-shine concrete that forms the floors, ceilings and walls of this very industrial space, these plants stand out like artworks in their own right. 'I like the greenness of them,' Ben says. 'They make a lovely contrast.'

The result of choosing such a pared-back palette, brought to life not by decoration, but by foliage, is an environment that invites serene contemplation. 'Being surrounded by so much concrete is very calming, actually,' Ben says. 'The tones here are very soft, so it all feels elegant and peaceful.' He bought the warehouse nine years ago, a single-storey structure with a corrugated steel roof, surrounded by terraced houses, and it took a further six years to meticulously design, plan and create its transformation. He enlisted the British architects Carmody Groarke, known for taking vast brutalist structures – both residential and public – and injecting them with warmth and vitality. He briefed them to stay close to the building's roots. 'I love solid things: I like things to have substance, to not be flimsy or thin. I was very keen on concrete and blue steel, and wanted the place to be industrial and tough. Partly because it is a warehouse, partly because I like this vibe, and partly because it's so dramatic and striking.' Using a few carefully curated plants to then soften the hard edges was always the plan. 'Without them, the house would be a bit bare, even for me,' Ben says.

He grew up in what he calls a messy home, and thinks this is why he is drawn to minimalism now. With his home stretching out over 370 square metres (4,000 square feet) and including four bedrooms, there is a lot of space left blank, but for the beguiling gleam of all that concrete. Every item that has made it into the house is carefully considered, from the cluster of mismatched dining chairs in the open-plan kitchen space, 'all of which are over twenty-five years old, because I thought it would be fun to nod to a bit of history', to the polished marble board in the concrete bath that serves as a surprisingly restful material to lie back on. Ben may have founded Metro Imaging, a business that produces and creates art, but his walls were left intentionally clear, to let the concrete be the true hero of the piece. And to allow the plants to stand out too, of course. 'I just don't like any that have frilly leaves,' he says – which, when taking into account all of his design choices, is very easy to believe.

Ben had the table specially made, and placed on wheels so it's easy to move around the space. The Dear Ingo ceiling light is from Moooi, and seating includes the Costes Chair by Philippe Starck and the Wiggle Side Chair by Vitra. The two-metre (six-foot) cactus nearby is just as structural as these modern design classics. The bar stools are from Viaduct, and the kitchen was designed by DOCA.

'Against the backdrop of smooth, polished-to-a-shine concrete that forms the floors, ceilings and walls of this very industrial space, these plants stand out like artworks in their own right.'

Previous Page: The low leather sofa from Living Divani sits beautifully against the height of the rubber plant and palm plants, which stand in matching glazed pots, their dark leaves contrasting with the concrete walls. The flamingo was found in a vintage store in Camden.

A banana leaf plant is the only sign of natural life in this otherwise very man-made space.

The leather flooring used here is the only nod to soft comfort in the house. The bed is by Desiree Ozium, and the bedside lamp is by Anglepoise.

The bathroom is also a stark space, with a single humidity-loving plant for solace; the taps and towel rail above and below the marble sink are from Vola.

Josh FitzGerald

Architect and co-founder of Archier
Hobart, Tasmania, Australia

THERE'S A FASCINATING CONTRAST at work in the design of Josh FitzGerald's cabin in the Tasmanian bush. The co-founder of architectural studio Archier created his home around the idea of temporality – it was built to stay on this spot for just five years, envisioned as a structure in a state of flux – and yet decorated only with plants because, Josh says, he is attracted to the fact they are anything but fleeting. 'I like the sense of time that a plant conveys: a monstera takes years, decades to grow to full height. Plants fight against the temporary nature of our lives and this home I've built, and that's why I'm drawn to them. They feel like they have a sense of permanence.'

The 53-square-metre (175-square-feet), single-level open-plan home Josh shares with his fiancée Millie and their two rescue greyhounds, Frankie and Rosie, was devised because they needed somewhere to live sooner than their budget would allow. The couple were trying to buy some land to build on, but the sale fell through. Nothing else was coming up in their price range, until Millie's father, a farmer, said they could have a corner of his acreage for five years: a perfect, shaded and secluded spot that was only 20 minutes from Hobart's city centre, and surrounded solely by native gum trees. And so Josh created a place to live that could be installed affordably and quickly – the prefabricated walls went up in the 40 minutes it took him to pop to the hardware store and back – and that could ultimately be moved on and adapted as time passed.

The walls and roof are made of SIPs (structurally insulated panels), lightweight boards that can be moved into and out of place easily. These are complemented by sandstone flooring and plenty of very strategically placed glass. 'You get your morning sun streaming in,' Josh says of the windows along one wall. 'It was quite daunting not having curtains at first, but we're in the middle of nowhere, no one can see in, and the landscape outside has been specifically planted to stop anyone who might walk past from just peering inside.' Fortunately, Josh and Millie are both early risers, and so the dawn light is a welcome feature.

The ethos of Josh's company, Archier, is to stay true to the materials. Most of Archier's projects are full of exposed materials because, Josh says, understanding what your space is made from helps you to nurture an emotional connection with your surroundings. His home takes that to the extreme, with the batch coding still streaming along the inside of the SIPs. 'I love the balance I've created between a mid-century modern aesthetic and the modernist principles of simplistic and lightweight materials,' Josh says. By 2022, Josh will have to pack this place up and rebuild it elsewhere, probably with an extra annexe or two on either end to create more space. While he's currently unsure of where it will be, one thing is a certainty – plants. 'I want foliage up and over the roof; I want monstera up to the ceiling. I want to watch them grow over time.' A very real way to put down roots in a home designed not to have any.

The island was made from spotted gum timber by a joiner who 'lived over the fence', and was designed to give the impression of 'a country farmhouse crossed with Japanese simplicity'. Cleverly, the area behind the island is recessed into the floor, meaning the island is the right height to stand at and cook on this side, and the perfect height to sit at on the other.

The flooring is made from sandstone, which Josh says is 'very tactile, encouraging you to walk around barefoot.' It warms up in the sun in a way other materials wouldn't, holding the heat in its ridges and grooves.

Partitioned from the living space only by a stud wall and some plants, the lack of privacy doesn't bother Josh and Millie, who regularly wear headphones in order to keep their noise to themselves.

The only area fully separated from the rest of the home, the bathroom is panelled by dimpled glass so that the banksia trees outside create an interesting interplay of shadow and light. 'It makes even brushing your teeth seem like an event,' Josh says.

Valentina Audrito

Architect, designer and co-founder of Word of Mouth
Hackney, London, UK

MOST OF THE PROJECTS WORKED ON by Word of Mouth – the architecture, interior design and art installation studio Valentina Audrito co-founded in 2006 – are in Bali. 'Designers have a lot of space to be themselves over there,' Valentina says. 'The island is full of very skilled craftsmen, so it's easy to experiment with materials, and the boundaries between inside and out are completely blurred. The Balinese connection with nature is very real.'

Word of Mouth's work is contemporary, based around clean lines, but given a fresh, organic feel by the way bright colours are juxtaposed with dazzling raw materials. It's an approach Valentina has brought back to her four-bedroom new build in London's Hackney, which she bought in 2017, just after the shell was finished by the previous owners and architects Liddicoat and Goldhill. 'I think rawness of materials can make a space warmer,' she says. This can be seen in her unpainted brick walls – 'so much more inviting than a plain white would be' – as well as the exposed wooden and metal beams that support the 3.6-metre-high (11.8-foot) ceilings. 'But what plants do is balance their hardness with a feeling of life.'

Plants are displayed just as proudly as the innards of the house: a mix of weeping figs, fiddle-leaf figs, palms and ferns. 'I chose ones that are aesthetically appealing to me, that have graphic shapes to their leaves,' Valentina says. 'It was important to me that some grow upwards and some climb down, so that there is variety in their form.' Having lived in Bali for 20 years, Valentina says that, without the plants, she'd really miss the sense of closeness to the natural world she fostered while living there. 'I think being surrounded by plants does enhance your way of life. They just make me feel healthier, both physically and mentally.'

The house is split over four floors, with the ground floor an entirely open space featuring a vast kitchen and dining area with a couple of steps up to a living room. Some of the principles of Balinese design have made their way into this space. 'In Bali, they believe in certain ways of circulation: in blocking some energies with walls and allowing others to flow by leaving rooms open.' Curtains in vividly bright hues separate the different zones, 'but only visually,' Valentina says. 'The advantages of having curtains instead of walls are that you perceive the space as one, as a whole, but you can still pull them across if you want privacy.'

Concrete – one of Valentina's favourite materials – stretches lavishly across the dining room floor, chosen for its smoothness underfoot. It was deliberately used for many of the plant holders, too. 'It looks good,' she says, 'to have the same material forging the connection between the house and the plants.'

The open-plan dining area is next to the kitchen and flooded with natural light. The 1950s chairs were found online, while the table is from Haus. The pendant lights and side table are both from Mad Atelier, and the curtain was made using Linara fabric by Romo. In the corner sit a palm plant and a fiddle-leaf fig.

The blue units were made to order by a local craftsman. Above the pans sit a mixture of monsteras and ferns.

'It feels great to be out here, among so much lush foliage,' Valentina says. The stool (used to prop open the door), table and lounge chairs are all from Made. Palm trees and ferns soften all the concrete.

Thickly carpeted stairs lead up to the living area, just off the dining area. The blue rug was made by Studio 65 – who happen to be Valentina's parents – and the coffee table is by Tom Dixon. A three metre (10 foot) weeping fig towers in the background.

The warmth of the red flooring is equalled by the legs of the planter, carefully chosen to connect it with the room. The bedside lamp is from Zara Home.

To the left of the bathroom, just off the
bedroom, is Valentina's office space, separated
by a curtain made from Linara fabric by Romo.

'While the tones found in raw materials bring warmth to a space, their hardness is balanced by the organic shapes and feel of the plants.'

Separated with a barn door, the bathroom is filled with light thanks to its high-up windows. The bath itself is bespoke, made using a tub from Bette. Next to the mirror sits a cloud-like fern, which enjoys the humidity of the room.

Brigette Romanek

Interior designer, founder of Romanek Design Studio
Laurel Canyon, Los Angeles, California, USA

'PEOPLE REMEMBER A FEELING,' says interior designer Brigette Romanek, 'far more than they remember how something looks. So that's the approach I take: to create spaces that are full of good vibes.' Nowhere is this more evident than in Brigette's own home, a 100-year-old Spanish-style villa in Laurel Canyon, in the north-west corner of Los Angeles, California. She bought it in 2014, and it was previously owned by the music producer Rick Rubin. The villa has hosted everyone from the Beatles to the Red Hot Chilli Peppers, and Brigette says that's all part of the history of the place she fell in love with. 'There is a real positive creativity here: those artists used to just come here and write, and you can still feel those uplifting vibes. The house has so many nuances, so many quirks, a real sense of culture and a great energy,' she says.

One of the quirks of the house comes from Brigette herself, in the form of indoor ficus trees that reach all the way to her double-height ceilings. 'I wanted people who come here to feel like they've been invited to a party,' Brigette says. 'By extending greenery all the way from the two-and-a-half acres of land that surround us to actually inside the home, there's a real sense of harmonious warmth – it goes beyond just an invitation to be here and actually makes you feel like you're part of something. My home isn't a museum: there are no velvet ropes. Plants bring life. They make you comfortable.'

As evidenced by the bold architectural shapes of the furniture Brigette has chosen, she likes pieces that make a statement – but each item has to relate to everything else in the room. 'Everything connects,' she says. 'Take the tree. If you start with that, everything around it has to be organic and soft in colour, to enhance the tree's natural beauty. My goal is that anywhere the eye goes, you're able to enjoy something that is beautiful. There is always a treat for the eye.'

The five-bedroom house needed quite a bit of renovation: the kitchen was just a tiny galley space; there was an old, creaky elevator (which Brigette turned into a powder room); and there was no air-conditioning system. But it was a case of working with what was here already. 'Some of the spaces had palatial wood floors, some marble, some terracotta, some wood panelling,' Brigette says. 'I wanted to keep these materials, which show how the house has aged over the years.' Set on a hill, far back from the road, the floor-to-ceiling windows are left bare, filling the large rooms with light. 'I love the Californian light [streaming in],' Brigette says. 'Its pinks and yellows. And with white walls, there is a real sense of harmony here.' She used 'about sixteen' different whites throughout the home – it depended on the room and its needs, and she doesn't feel there was one catch-all white that would work everywhere – but is particularly fond of Benjamin Moore's Decorator's White and Farrow & Ball's All White, for their pure, refreshing brightness. 'I feel invigorated when I'm home,' Brigette says. 'You shut the gates to the outside world, you grab a glass of wine, head to the den and marvel at the greenery that surrounds you. Put simply, being here is just heaven.'

Painted in All White by Farrow & Ball, the large living area is home to a very impressive ficus tree. 'That was my starting point, and everything around it feels organic, too,' Brigette says. The chaise is by Hans Wegner, the bench is by Poul Kjærholm, and the pendant lights are from Apparatus Studio. The chair is by Faye Toogood, and the coffee table is by Gae Aulenti.

'People remember a feeling far more than they remember how something looks.'

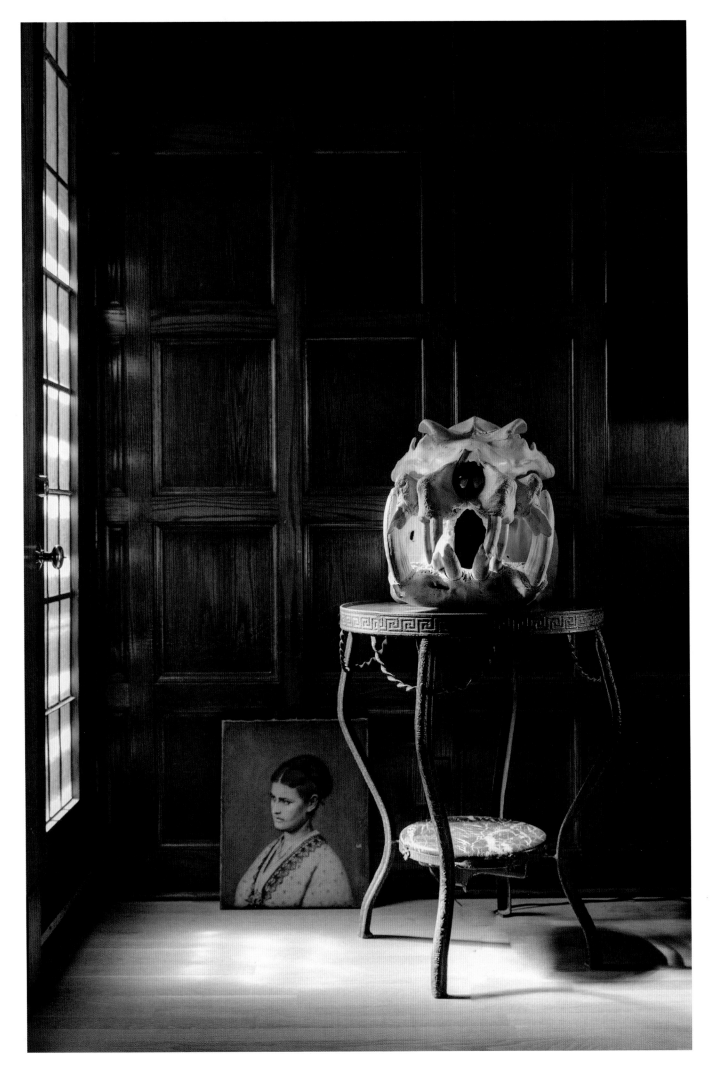

Overleaf: The windows are left uncovered in order to flood the space with the Californian light Brigette loves so much. The chandelier is from Apparatus Studio, and the dining table and bench were custom made.

Nick Douwma and Kara Melchers

Music producer and furniture designer,
De Beauvoir, Hackney, London, UK

FURNITURE DESIGNER KARA MELCHERS CAN track her life in monsteras. The early Victorian terrace house that she shares with her music producer partner Nick Douwma is full of them: they stand majestically in corners of the living room and bathroom, and on kitchen shelves. They're all cuttings from one original plant, that she dubbed 'Mama Cheese', and have moved with Kara through various flats and homes as she has built a life in the city, learning to propagate along the way. 'They grow with you,' Kara says. 'Plants give you something to nurture, and having another living thing in your home truly makes it a nicer environment.' Having grown up in the countryside, her plants have helped her feel grounded in the city. 'The more you can bring the outside in, the more calming your space will feel,' Kara says.

Creating a tranquil environment was the goal of the total renovation the couple undertook of this three-storey, flat-fronted house in De Beauvoir, a leafy area of Hackney, London. They enlisted Joe Magri at HUT Architects to gut the house, extend the kitchen and throw the space open with skylights and internal glass walls, with the aim of flooding their home with a wellness-inducing brightness. 'We found overselves drawn to more natural, organic colours when we were doing the project' Nick says. 'Browns and beiges and greens. In 2017 it seemed blues were everywhere in renovations we saw, but this earthier, warmer palette felt more unusual.'

The Douglas Fir hallway and staircase are the first things you see as you walk through the door, and set the tone for the aesthetic. 'Because the fir trees themselves are so big, they create huge planks,' Nick says, explaining why they look almost seamless. The jutting banister is also made of sheets of Douglas Fir

pressed together, resulting in a sharp architectural detail that still seems soft to the eye. Terrazzo features prominently too – in the bathroom floor and the fireplace in the living room – but when you look closely, the fireplace, made by the Liverpool-based company Granby workshop, isn't all that it seems. 'It's a unique type of terrazzo they make from recycled building rubble, which is then smoothed off to create a flat surface' Kara says. 'The colours this produces really pop against the white walls.'

During the course of the building work, the outside space was razed, so Nick and Kara commissioned garden designer Tom Massey to help them create a new space from scratch. it seems to glow outside the kitchen extension, a literal urban jungle. 'I love big, prehistoric-looking plants,' Nick says. 'Tree ferns, echiums and climbers fill the view. If you're going to add a big window to the back of the house, it's important to think about what you'll be looking out at.' The foliage is complemented by the kitchen cabinets, made by British standard and painted in invisible Green by Little Greene, and the result is a renovation that creates a real sense of airiness in a building that was originally quite dark and confined, built almost 200 years ago for large families to inhabit together. With its glass inner partitions, walls painted in Farrow & Ball's All White and structural plants in every corner, the house now feels airy, fresh and a calm space in a busy city. 'We really thought about the flow,' Nick says, explaining how the eye travels easily throughout the home, unbothered by too much obstruction. 'And how the design now allows light to come into every corner of the house.'

Previous page: The living room is separated from the hall by a glass door, allowing a sense of openness to pervade the ground-floor layout. The sofa is from Love Your Home, and ceiling light is by Lambert and Fils. The white chair and black lamp arc both by &Tradition. The table is the design classic by Isamu Noguchi, now in production by Vitra.

The fireplace surround isn't actually terrazzo, but a terrazzo-style material, made of rubble and old bricks by Granby Workshop.

'They grow with you. Plants give you something to nurture, and having another living thing in your home truly makes it a nicer environment.'

Both the stairs and banister are made from Douglas Fir,
with its large planks creating a seamless and soothing effect.

The terrazzo floor creates a striking contrast with another of Kara's monsteras. The Stand bathtub is by Norm Architects.

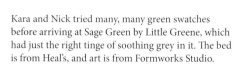

Kara and Nick tried many, many green swatches before arriving at Sage Green by Little Greene, which had just the right tinge of soothing grey in it. The bed is from Heal's, and art is from Formworks Studio.

Kara made the bench herself, for her furniture brand Uncommon Ancestor. 'I'm interested in how thin I can make things, but how they can still be strong,' she says of the slim metal frame.

Looking out on to the back garden, the open-plan dining area in the kitchen extension is light and bright, painted in Farrow & Ball's All White. The dining table is by Skagerak and chairs are vintage teak Jason Chairs by Carl Jacobs. A rubber plant grows happily in the corner.

The cabinets were made by British Standard and painted in Little Greene's Invisible Green. The worktops are marble and the tap is from Dornbracht. The handles were made bespoke by a local ironmonger.

Juliana Campello

Veterinarian
São Paulo, Brazil

'I NEED TO FEEL NATURE, TO FEEL outside,' Juliana Campello says. 'To feel that I'm not locked inside.' It's a difficult request for someone who lives in a city as built up as São Paulo, Brazil, but an ethos that she folded into the design of her home near the city centre. It was a crumbling 1940s house in a part of town filled with surprisingly low-rise buildings – much of São Paulo is towers – and allowed Juliana to have a vision of an indoor/outdoor way of life. Working with the architect Lucio Fleury she installed glass panels in the roof that 'mean you can look up and see airplanes in the day and the moon at night' and glass doors that shutter open to allow the family to wander in and out as if they were part of the same thing.

'The idea was to blur the lines between what was the outside, and what was in,' Juliana says, having knocked down almost every wall and using the Brazilian wood Cumaru as both the decking on the terrace and for the interior flooring. 'I wanted to have wood on the floor so that we could make a skate path that the kids could cycle their bikes on around the house, pass through the middle of the living area and back to to outside. It was just meant to be fun, to soften what it's like to live in a city.' The idea evolved into a run of black and white tiles that snakes through the living area, neatly zoning the open plan kitchen and living space, and giving the children a run to wheel across. 'We realised tiles would be easier to wash and clean than wood,' Juliana says.

Plants trail across the wooden decking and inside the house too. It's a verdant, leafy jungle mix of monstera, ficus and other tropical plants like banana leaf and palms and, like the tiles, their existence is more than just decorative. 'They make me feel like I have contact with nature,' Juliana says. 'But more than that, caring for them gives me a sense of routine, a connection to the world.' The daily habits of watering those that need it, pruning where required and just general maintenance of this living part of her decor aids a bit of mindfulness in an otherwise busy life as a veterinarian. 'To have plants successfully, you have to connect with them,' Juliana says. 'People come and visit and say they'd like to have the same plants as me, but I know every leaf, I look at them and really see them. With a plant you build a relationship – you don't just water it once a week but you learn to know when it needs to be done. It's because they give you the chance to build a connection.'

The kitchen is made from Cumaru veneers, the same wood as used for the floors. 'We thought that the yellow would be a really cheerful contrast to the wood,' Juliana says. It is flanked by a strip of black and white tiles that runs through the house and round the outside, creating a perfect loop for the kids to use as a skatepark.

With the beguiling patina of cement, the wall is actually painted in a special textured clay paint, which gives the same effect.

It was the architect Lucio Fleury's idea to keep the structural engineered steal beams exposed, making a feature of them rather than covering them. 'And I like the honesty of that, of being able to see how the building stands,' Juliana says.

Fi Lindsay

Co-founder of HueHome
Wiltshire, UK

THE DESIGN OF FI'S HOME, IN THE British countryside, all revolves around its relationship to nature. 'Everything here is about looking out the window at the changing skies,' Fi says. With nothing but the undulating hills of Wiltshire seen beyond the glass wall, Fiona's total refurbishment of a derelict barn, and the former farmyard it sat in, was carried out with the natural world in mind. 'There was nothing here,' Fiona says of the site she bought in 2014, her house the only barn of several once here that was not pulled down. 'With the removal of the metal agricultural buildings that had covered much of the land there was a fantastic opportunity to attract wildlife.' She planted wild flowers which, over time, has caused a diversity of birds, frogs and other creatures. 'There are now barn owls again – I imagine they lived in the barn once upon a time – and they've returned to the boxes we put up.'

Having moved from London to get closer to greenery, nature is prized equally highly inside the home. Designed with Ange Howell, Fi's business partner and co-founder of their interiors product brand HueHome, it was created as a minimalist canvas in front of which indoor plants as big as trees could stand out. 'The whole place is painted in a standard white matt, there was no way I'd use anything else in such a large space,' Fi says. 'The patterns the plants make against the walls as the sun goes down are so fascinating, so beautiful.' A Ficus

Benjamina that Fi estimates is nearly eight metres (26 feet) tall towers in a textural pot, while a smaller – but still large – Kentia palm lives nearby.

Of course, the size of the plants is made possible by the large space, which Fi admits was a challenge to know how to decorate. At over 400 square metres (1,300 square feet), Fi says it would have been 'fine for skateboarding, but harder to live in! It felt a bit like a warehouse, and we needed to soften it considerably, with texture and earthy, simple decor.' To break up the space – all of which is on one level except her office, on an open mezzanine at one end – she built the central fireplace which can be seen from both sides, causing a sensation of zoning but not closing off the room entirely. She was never tempted to put walls or another storey into the barn. 'The building's integrity would be gone,' she says. 'I wanted to be able to see the frame of what it was before.'

Original beams vault the ceiling, standing in one side, while the bricks were painted white so the wood stood out. The flooring was concrete, crafted by Lazenby, which, Fi says 'is most similar to what was once here.' Light streams in, the effect Fi wanted. "It's so quiet and peaceful here,' she says, a mood enhanced by her serene design choices. There is just one aspect she'd change. 'I'd have more plants if I could,' Fi says. 'But it's the scale of the ones I have, growing on their own, which makes them really stand out.'

Previous page: Separated from the dining area by the fireplace, the living area is overseen by a large Ficus Benjamina. The sofas are from HAY.

Made from oak, the four-metre-long (13-foot-long) Silas dining table is by Tom Hitchen, available from HueHome. 'It gets a lot of wear and tear from the family, but it's very robust,' Fi says. It is surrounded by Wishbone chairs, while the pendant light above it is by Davey Lighting.

'The patterns the
plants make against
the walls as the
sun goes down
are so fascintating,
so beautiful.'

The only dark part of the house, the main bedroom is painted in Pavilion Grey by Farrow and Ball. 'It's a softer shade than we've used everywhere else, and is lovely to wake up to,' Fi says. The bed is from Loaf, and pendant light from Habibi.

Ben Allen

Architect and founder of Studio Ben Allen
Bethnal Green, London, UK

'The plants provide a sense of enclosure, and a connection to the outside world. Noticing how the shadows they form change throughout the day, how the light catches them at different times of the morning and afternoon, is one of the most satisfying aspects of the home, helping me feel at one with the passing of the sun.'

FOR ARCHITECT BEN ALLEN, DESIGN is all about a meticulous choice of materials, and basing that choice around what will best promote wellness in the people who come into contact with his work. He believes that our surroundings can greatly affect how we feel, from the physical – the right amount of natural light helping to boost serotonin and promote better sleep through the enhancement of our circadian rhythms – to more abstract elements of wellbeing. 'So many buildings are dishonest,' he says. 'They hide foams and glues and resins behind walls and in joints, and are made up of materials that the average person can't understand. If you can't comprehend your surroundings, you can't feel connected to them; and if you can't feel connected, you can't truly respect the space around you. Ultimately, you feel more grounded and happier in your life if you know what your space is made of.'

It's an interesting philosophy, and one that sees Ben's own apartment – a split-level two-bed on the tenth and eleventh floors of a 1950s tower block designed by Sir Denys Lasdun – filled with untreated timber, poured rubber flooring, and plenty of plants stacked on the trellis dividers that semi-separate the kitchen-dining space from the living area. 'Up here in the sky, it can be bright when the sun comes out, but on a grim London day, you can need a bit of help to feel comforted,' Ben says. 'The plants provide a sense of enclosure, and a connection to the outside world. Noticing how the shadows they form change throughout the day, how the light catches them at different times of the morning and afternoon, is one of the most satisfying aspects of the home, helping me feel at one with the passing of the sun.'

Ben's work includes both residential and commercial projects: an office space he designed in Birmingham was the first in the UK to receive WELL Building Standard certification from the International WELL Building Institute, meaning the space will enhance the health of those who use it. 'Fully open-plan spaces are never good for well-being, as they make us feel exposed,' Ben says. 'Similarly, small areas can make us feel trapped. Plant dividers provide the best of both worlds: the safety of enclosure, but the freedom of still being able to see who or what is in the zone next to you.' He only uses materials that will age well, and that have one colour all the way through, so that if they are chipped, they still look beautiful rather than tired. Damaged surroundings are another factor Ben thinks can contribute to a general feeling of malaise. 'Things like melamine may be affordable and practical, but once the surface gets damaged, it looks terrible,' he says. 'You then start to feel worse about your surroundings, and you stop taking care of them. You lose pride in your home, which can have a negative effect on your sense of self.' Consequently, the concrete worktop in Ben's kitchen is dyed all the way through with copper, creating a vivid green tinge that is constant even in its core, while the blue of the Valchromat panels used to form his workspace runs right through the material, too.

Ben recommends choosing plants that are a lighter, brighter green, as 'dark green leaves are not very biophilic – they can feel pretty bleak on a winter's day'. He also encourages embracing foliage in its many forms. 'Humans are natural collectors,' he says. 'And the more distinctive and personal to yourself you make your environment, the more likely you are to identity with your space. To feel happy about where you are.'

Separated from the kitchen by an oak trellis, an artfully chosen monstera, a Japanese money plant and some ivy, this is where Ben works, reads and contemplates. The stool is from Another Country and the sofa is by Robin Day for Habitat. It's flanked by a Benjamina parlour palm and a ficus.

Books are as important to Ben as plants, with both providing hints about the personality of the homeowner. The string of hearts plant drapes lovingly over several spines.

The glass bottles catch the light just as beautifully as the plants, and are a mix of Jasper Conran designs for Cappellini and vintage flea market finds.

Reconfigured kitchen cabinets were given new life with bespoke tri-ply doors in solid oak. The tiles are from Villeroy & Boch, and the green worktop is concrete pigmented with copper. The blue and red pots are Danish designs from the 1950s.

The John Lewis bed has been enhanced by a panel from
Kvadrat, which is used as a headboard. The cupboards are
made from larch, and the mirrored shelves are bespoke.

Adrian and Megan Corrigall

Commercial diver,
Lewes, Sussex, UK

ON A WARM SUMMER'S DAY, WHEN the windows of Adrian Corrigall's home are wide open, the gentle, leafy scents of the dwarf palms, phormiums, Canary Island date palms, yuccas and grasses drift in from where they're planted around the pool. They mingle, creating a gentle ambience, one of the many considerations Adrian has made to soften the hard edges of his countryside concrete lair, a place where the mood is set always, in his words, to 'monastic'.

'You don't paint a white wall and say "that's my décor"', Adrian says. 'Concrete is the same. Yes, it's what the house is made of, but it's a canvas with which to make a cocoon, not the cocoon itself.' Inspired by the conservatory at London's Barbican, a brutalist monument, plants cascade over three-quarter-height partitions that separate the kitchen and dining area, creating an indoor jungle. Elsewhere, doors were removed because Adrian 'finds them too hard' and replaced with soft black velvet curtains, while jewel-bright pieces of furniture glow against their rich, dark backdrop. The result is a home so acoustically clever, so calming and genteel, that Adrian says people can move around it silently. 'Everyone looks at a home like this and thinks visually, but we started with how it sounded, its tactility and smell, the interplay of light around it, how we could use it to create a place of comfort and warmth.' Even the concrete itself isn't as hard-looking as might be expected. 'We've polished the whole building, adding a satin resin, and that makes the surfaces pop,' Adrian says. 'This brings up all the tones, exposes the clouds in the concrete and makes it look like natural stone. Yes, it's an engineered product, but it forms naturally and in its own way when you pour it, creating air bubbles, little dots, and that makes it all seem more … mellow.'

The four-bedroom home in Lewes, Sussex, has four-metre- (13-foot-) high ceilings and looks out on the South Downs. Adrian completed it in 2020, replacing the bungalow that previously sat here. It's a revolutionary structure, made with techniques never seen before in the UK. Adrian had always loved concrete, growing up in Scotland and thinking that concrete skate parks were infinitely cool, and his background in design made him want to push the process as far as he could. 'I reckon we saved £98,000 ($135,000) by getting rid of rebars,' he says. Instead, the advanced fibre-reinforced Resilia concrete he used was designed by Mexican company CEMEX to grip on to itself, not the normally required rebars in a building. This creates a clean spread through the environmentally friendly mix and means the concrete supports its own weight. Adrian's home was the first building in the world built with in this material. 'The downside was it was very difficult to pump, and saw me put in endless nineteen-hour days,' Adrian says. 'but I wanted to move boundaries, to create something new. PERI provided the formwork we used to cast the concrete. It's a revolutionary system of recycled, and fully recyclable, plastic formwork. Waste in this area traditionally is horrific, so for us this product was a phenomenal discovery.'

Concrete and plants, Adrian says, work so well together that 'it's a no brainer!' As with his brightly coloured furniture, the vivid green of the philodendrons, Chinese money plants and palms shine from their dark surroundings. Adrian likes how they change and grow: not always perfect, adding character. 'There's a joy in imperfection in a home that feels handmade rather than manmade,' Adrian says. 'We left pencil-mark measurements on the walls on purpose, as they provide a reference for how the space was made, and in certain spots, you can see the fingerprints of the makers. I love that sense of the story.'

A four-metre (13-foot) high Strelitzia reaches the ceiling: this is Adrian's first indoor tree, and one of which he's particularly proud. The oak table was given to him by a friend, and the vintage chairs are by the mid-century company Kandya. The pendant light was an old Parisian street lamp. Next to the dining area, spiderworts and Monstera adansonii creep over from a planter on top of the partition to the kitchen, inspired by the conservatory at London's Barbican.

'The vivid green of the philodendrons, Chinese money plants and palms shine from their dark surroundings.'

The worktop is made of micro-cement, a very thin
concrete. Adrian says he finds the process of working
it into place 'very cathartic'.

The bedroom looks out to the pool, and the only reason it doesn't feature plants is because Adrian hasn't got round to adding them yet. The bed is from B&B Italia.

The sliding doors – the only rooms in the house to have
doors are the bathrooms – are made from Forescolor,
a wood fibreboard that is coloured throughout.

The pool is ten metres long (32 feet) and three metres
(10 feet) deep, with a base of black resin, chosen
'so that it feels bottomless,' Adrian says. It's heated,
and surrounded by dwarf palms, phormiums,
Canary Island date palms, yuccas and some grasses,
all of which have a gentle fragrance that can softly
float into the house.

Robert Storey

Founder and head of spatital design agency Storey Studio
Dalston, London, UK

AS THE HEAD OF STOREY STUDIO, a spatial design agency that has created installations, windows and exhibitions for brands like Hermes, Nike and Prada, Robert Storey likes to take people on a journey. In fact, in perhaps the case of the strongest nominative determinism ever, he wants to design rooms that tell a story. 'I want people to walk in and forget what has happened to them before, to be amazed,' he says. 'My favourite thing is when their first word is "wow". I think design can take you away from everything else, immerse you in an exact moment, and change the way you feel.'

In a quieter way than the sets he designs, his house has the same ethos too. A mostly white walled conversion of the top half of a Victorian terrace, the idea was that it would be decorated like a gallery space, a blank backdrop against which Robert's furniture – and plants – would stand out. 'The reason I decided to paint everything white was that it was my strategy to bring colour in elsewhere,' he says, adding that he is fascinated by the interplay and relationship different colours and shapes have between them. 'I love colour. I love it so much. When I enter the living room I feel like I'm walking into an orchestra of different colours, the furniture is all singing harmoniously to me. The Yves Klein blue sofa and the bright, pure yellow chairs, brought together by the rug that picks up both shades. It's a symphony, really, the way they balance together.'

A self-confessed minimalist, most of the decorative pieces in Robert's home are plants. 'I don't have a lot of objects in the house but I love how incredible it is that we have all these different species of plants, plants whose sculptural forms have inspired pretty much everything mankind has created,' Robert says. 'You can fill your home with these wonderful, natural beings, and be brought so much joy by them.

There is so much detail in a plant you can sit and stare at them for an hour or two, feeling more and more at peace with the tranquility they create.' Being able to feel a connection to nature is one of the most important parts of life for Robert, who grew up in an idyllic-sounding country childhood filled with treehouse-making and dam-building. 'Me bringing plants in, that's me bringing in myself,' Robert says. One of his most treasured collections is the pine cones on the shelf behind his bed, collected on walks in various forests throughout the years. 'I love the simplicity of not needing to buy a souvenir, but to be able to pick up a pine cone and have that as a sentimental memory,' he says. 'I know where each cone has come from, I remember finding each one. They chart my life, my childhood, my family and bring them all into my surrounding in the city.'

Their backdrop may be kept simple, but the renovation process was anything but. Having been rented out for years, when Robert bought his home in 2018 it was in disrepair, last decorated in the 1980s. he took down every wall, took up every floor and ceiling, and lovingly rewired and reinsulated, putting back each wall where it had been, each floorboard tenderly in its place. 'I really wanted to celebrate what the house had been, to strip the building back to what it was,' Robert says. 'But just make it new again, give it live for the next generation while singing in its original way.' He added ornate coving back in, found Victorian doors to replace the flat ones that had been installed at some point, and then added a few contemporary flourishes. 'When you interweave carpentry that is designed in a current way, like the kitchen and bedroom cabinets, there is another form of balance at work,' Robert says. A design language, that, when used by him, like the furniture, it sings.

Previous page: One of the changes Robert made to the layout was making the hallway double height. It became the perfect spot to hang a cluster of vintage opaline pendant lights from the Netherlands.

Designed by Robert himself, the kitchen was made by his friend Otis Poole-Evans of Craftwork. It is made from Fenix, a laminated plywood that is scratch and stain proof. "A brilliant material," Robert says. The stools are from John Lewis.

Surrounded by plants, Robert says he could stare at
them for hours. The floorboards are lovingly restored,
found under the 1980s carpet he inherited, and
the Melting Pot table is by Dirk van der kooij.
The dining chairs are by Hans Wegner and art by
Andrej Dúbravský.

The cabinets were made by Craftowrks, designed by Robert. 'I didn't want any handles, or anyhitng that wasn't simple,' he says. The collection of pine cones above the bed connects Robert to nature in the same way as his plants. The art is by Albert Riera Galceran.

The white walls, painted in Farrow & Ball's Dimpse, are the perfect backdrop to let the block primary colours of the furniture stand out. The yellow chairs are by Finn Juhl, the sofa by Eric Rasmussen for Paustian, the glass coffee table by Richard Young for Merrow Associates and ceiling light is by Gaetano Sciolari. 'I love the way the metal of the table speaks to the metal of the chandelier,' Robert says. The sculptural oak floor lamp was designed by Robert, and made by his father.

Millie and Dave Wells

Environmental advisor and CEO of a not-for-profit sports programme
Warrandyte, Melbourne, Australia

TO THOSE UNFAMILIAR WITH Warrandyte, these photos of Millie and Dave Wells' home there implies it's deep in the Australian bush. Surrounded by wattles and gum trees, their house appears to peek out of a dense jungle. It is, however, just 30 minutes from Melbourne's city centre, in a 'green wedge' area designated by the government to ensure the city has access to rich foliage.

Its proximity to town doesn't make it any less exotic, though. Kangaroos occasionally hop down the path, echidnas have been spotted in the chicken coop, and parrots and cockatoos flit between the trees.

Inside, the 12,000-square-metre (39,000-square-foot) detached two-storey home is equally filled with vegetation. 'We had a joke with the builders that when they had finished an area, we'd say, "It looks good, but it's missing something – plants!"' Millie says. She works in environmental policy for local government, and her role is focused on making sure everyone in Melbourne has trees, nature and vegetation around them. As well as this being an answer to climate change, providing tree canopies as shade in areas that suffer from heatwaves, there is an emotional reason, too. 'Research shows that people who live in green areas are more positive; that there is a restorative power in looking at plants,' Millie says. 'Just being able to see nature has a calming and rejuvenating effect on my mind, and my soul too.'

This explains the strings of pearls that drape from every shelf, the peace lilies that bloom and the monsteras that tower in every corner of her architecturally fascinating home. It's all designed to be as open-plan as possible, so that, as Dave says, 'When you open up all the doors, you can be quite deep in the house and still feel engaged with the outside.'

The exterior of the house is dark, painted in Grid by Dulux, so that, as Millie says, 'When you approach our home, the greenery surrounding it stands out more. Inside has the reverse effect: the frames of the window are dark, and that helps draw the eye out to the plant life outside.' The house had been built in 2001 but was gloomy and not conducive to hosting, Millie says, so the couple worked with local builders Sanctum Homes, whose director, Hamish White, focuses on creating high-performing, sustainable homes. A lot of thought was put into airflow, and, unusually for Australia, the windows are double-glazed in order to keep the home well insulated against the sun.

Inside, the timber ceiling and wood floors are left exposed, to enhance that feeling of being encased by natural materials, but almost every other surface is smooth, polished and white. 'We wanted things to be simple and clean-cut, so that when you have signs of life, like plants, they really do take on their own vibrancy,' Millie says. 'If you took them away, the house would be naked,' says Dave.

The wrap-around terrace separates the home from its garden, where blood orange, mandarin and grapefruit trees grow. The hanging chair is from Byron Bay Hanging Chairs, and the dining set was made by Lee Gratton of Gratton Design.

The hanging planter box is by Gratton of Gratton
design, and is full of hanging monstera and ferns.

The quartz worktop was made by Caesarstone, and the tap, from Faucet Strommen, was chosen because it reminded Millie of a garden tap. The tiles are Spanish, and the stools were found on Gumtree. 'It's my ethos to recycle and reuse and give things an extended life,' Millie says.

A large rubber plant continues the vegetation
theme upstairs, chosen for its ability to thrive in
lower light. The table lamp is from Kmart.

Anna Liu and Mike Tonkin

Architects and directors of Tonkin Liu
Clerkenwell, London, UK

'WE WANT ALL OF OUR PROJECTS TO connect to nature: it's like a mantra to us,' says Anna Liu from her home in the handsome central London neighbourhood of Clerkenwell. 'Everything in architecture can be influenced by nature, from the largest cityscape echoing the mountains to the round shape of a door handle evoking a shell. We want to bring nature into our buildings, to celebrate it.'

In fact, the work she produces with her husband and partner Mike Tonkin is directly shaped by what they have seen in the natural world, from bridges that twist and curve and corrugate like molluscs, as strong as the sea creatures they emulate, to a house by the coast with a gently undulating roof that complements the nearby waves. Their most recent work is on the Tower of Light, which has just been completed in Manchester: a 40-metre- (130-foot-) high tower made of steel just six millimetres thick, holding up the five flues for a new green energy centre. It looks a little like an upside down water droplet splashing as it hits a surface.

In their own home, a listed four-storey Georgian townhouse, a vast basement extension – which required a full excavation – includes an extravagantly looping, almost key-hole shaped hole in the roof called 'Sun Rain Rooms', through which rain pours beautifully over a sedum roof and onto the stone courtyard and into the rain water collection tank below. It was completed in 2017 after winning the appeal in 2008. The appeals board agreed that it was more than architecture: in the planning inspectorate's words, 'a kind of jeu d'esprit': an architectural and landscaping project that plays with the idea of what a modern small urban garden may be.

The roof is made from several layers of plywood, and the ridges in the underside of the skylights were added not just for aesthetic value (because they reflect the ripples of the rain in the living, lily-filled water tank below), but because they structurally transfer the weight at the point where the beams in the roof cross one another.

Anna says being enveloped in this structure is akin to a religious experience. 'Plants fill me with a sense of wonder,' she says, explaining that she particularly likes the durability of succulents. 'Their different structures are amazing: they are always changing and just quietly doing what they do. Looking at them actually fills with me with awe.'

The interior of the home is less verdant, but no less considered. Every wall is covered in white, so, Anna says, 'our personality comes through in other things, such as in the colours of our spices in the kitchen, our art, our friends' clothes. We try and persuade all our clients to make their spaces white for the same reason. White is a context for life to live out in front of.' The home feels minimal but detailed: there are treasured items everywhere, but they feel very curated. 'I once took a poetry course, and the teacher said if a word wasn't giving you five different feelings, don't use it. Design is the same: everything we choose, we do so because it serves a purpose.'

The spice racks were designed by Mike and made from old chipboard found on the street. 'We like to use affordable materials, but get the best from them,' Anna says, having added beeswax to their corners to strengthen them. The flooring is from Dinesen.

Running along the side of the basement extension, but under cover, is the perfect place to sit and contemplate nature, with succulents hanging above it. 'I like them because they can take my lack of care,' Anna jokes.

At the end of the walkway, a Super Elliptical table by Fritz Hansen is surrounded by Panton chairs. It's outdoors, and this is where Anna sits to have dinner in the summer, looking back at the house.

Be, a Silken Windhound, sits on a black sofa from Habitat in front of bookshelves from Vitsœ. A ficus bends over the edge of the sofa. 'I'm drawn to leafy plants. I think it speaks to my background, growing up in the tropics of Taiwan,' says Anna.

Opposite the fireplace, some dried leaves are reflected in the mirror, positioned as art in their own right. 'Even in an urban garden, you can find such variety in the shape of leaves,' Anna says. 'They're a family of things that relate to each other, which is how we like to approach design.'

'I once took a poetry course, and the teacher said if a word wasn't working in five different ways, don't use it. Design is the same: we want to achieve the most with the least. Every part of our design has to work really hard in multiple ways, socially, structurally, environmentally, experientially.'

Lars Richardson

Restaurateur and owner of Thirsty Bear microbrewery
Sebastopol, California, USA

LARS RICHARDSON, DANISH-BORN restaurateur and microbrewery owner, describes his adopted home of Sebastopol as a 'hippy outpost'. An hour north of San Francisco, California, and in the wine country of Sonoma County, he calls the small rural town a 'progressive hub': an influx of creatives who moved here from the city have brought with them an artistic flavour. And perhaps there is nothing more brilliantly 'free love' than creating a tropical garden inside your home and allowing a chirruping troupe of tree frogs to live there with you, too. 'Every evening, as the sun goes down, all these frogs start talking to us while we're having dinner,' Lars says. 'You're eating, surrounded by candlelight, and you hear them chatting. It's quite magical.'

The home Lars shares with his artist wife, Laila Carlsen – and those frogs – was once a barn and is actually his holiday home, with his main place of residence being the farmhouse out the back, where they spend weeknights. They come down to the converted barn (which is also Laila's studio) at weekends to host intimate concerts, dinners with friends and theatrical events outside. Designed by Casper Mork-Ulnes of Mork Ulnes Architects, it was inspired by the theory behind biospheres. 'I like the idea of these big globes in which you can grow tropical plants and literally bring the outside in,' Lars says. The original plans for the new structure (the barn that had been here was condemned and torn down) were all glass, but this was eventually deemed both expensive and impractical. 'It's not so conducive to outdoor living here, as it gets cold in the winter, so instead we had big sliding doors built across the front of the barn, which in the summer we can just open. Animals flood in – they can't tell if it's indoors or outdoors, so birds sit in the living rooms, our chickens wander about. It's just the way we live.'

The animals' confusion arises from the home's most notable feature, the plant life. Vast banana plants, avocado trees, fern trees, fig trees, taro and bamboo grow out of cut-ins in the concrete floor, giant indoor flower beds in which foliage seems to flourish. Lars has managed to replicate the conditions of the plants' natural habitats, with the concrete being as cool as the forest floor at midnight, yet with sunlight beating through the glass doors and ceilings to warm it up during the day. The roof was created in a butterfly shape so as to 'give us large areas of wall space in which to hang art up to the ceiling,' with the concrete an ideal neutral backdrop to the couple's artwork. The build was an unusual process. The walls were formed by shooting layers of fast-drying concrete on to old planks rescued from the barn that had once stood here, with the crew sanding it down and smoothing it out on the inside as they went. Then, once they had a rigid structure, the wood was pulled off what was now the outside of the building, leaving behind the texture of its grain – 'which we're so happy about,' Lars says. 'It turns a hard substance into something much more inviting.'

Lars uses the same adjective to describe how the plants make this space feel. 'The vegetation changes every time I walk in. I needed to cut some down yesterday, as the vines were reaching right into the kitchen.' Creepers bring bare walls to life: an ever-evolving art installation, a living version of the gallery walls Laila has created – and swaps around almost as much – in the back room. 'We're all over the place as far as our collecting goes,' Lars says. 'There is no "red line" that connects what we have: it's just a hotchpotch really, a wonderful mishmash of styles.' In art, and in plant life, too.

'Animals flood in – they can't tell if it's indoors or outdoors, so birds sit in the living rooms, our chickens wander about.'

Just inside the glass doors the table, reclaimed from Lars' brewery, is surrounded by vegetation, in which the tree frogs live, serenading diners as they eat. 'They're chameleon, on the white concrete they turn greyish, on the plant they turn a kind of green.' The chairs are from Restoration Hardware.

Lars and Laila's art collection in the living area constantly changes. The space has impressively high walls thanks to the butterfly roof. The coffee table and sofas were brought over by Lars from Norway, and the staircase leads up to Laila's studio.

Made out of reclaimed wood by the
acclaimed arborist and sawyer Evan Shively,
the kitchen tends to get overrun by vines.

Barbara Weiss

Architect and founder of Barbara Weiss Architects
Westminster, London, UK

'PLANTS SOFTEN EVEN THE MOST RIGID OF architectural lines and tie everything together,' says architect Barbara Weiss, founder of her eponymous architectural practice known for its detailing and timeless design. 'They're essential in bringing life to all sorts of spaces. What thrills me most, however, is the infinite variety of leaf shapes, and the endless combinations one can achieve: the thin little cactus next to the flat leaves of a fig, the sculptural quality of how they interact. It's all about getting that perfect tension of contrasting colours, textures and patterns.' Every piece of Barbara's home is this considered, part of a pain-staking process that took five years from purchasing a most unusual property to bringing it together before moving in. Each detail of her large and comfortable house in London's Westminster, converted from a 1920s pub which had subsequently been turned into offices, was chosen and designed meticulously. Central to it all, a new, strikingly sculptural staircase, referencing a very specific moment in architectural history, with its bronze handrail inspired by a similar steel one at the Fondation Le Corbusier in Paris. While the old stair was hidden away in a remote corner of the building, this one, with its gentle risers and generous treads, is an important feature and real pleasure to use, each floor dedicated to a different display, whether old maps, Bauhaus art or, at the top of the house, of a variety of interesting plants.

There is nothing stark about Barbara's house, which is both open-plan and upside down, with the living spaces at the top of the building and the bedrooms downstairs. Having trained as an architect in the 1970s, there are nods everywhere, throughout the house, to her professional background, from the white walls – 'During my training, architects only worked with white and black… colours on the whole were frowned upon'– to the giant avocado tree which, incredibly, Barbara grew from a pip eight years ago.

'Many of my early architect friends were growing avocado trees at that time, it was quite competitive'– she says simply of the plant, which now reaches from the living area up to the mezzanine level above. It shimmers in the sunlight of the vast windows: windows Barbara fought the planners to get permission for, to bring light and character to the double-height living space – against their more traditional preference for windows getting smaller towards the top of buildings.

Both the avocado tree and Barbara benefit from a lot of light. 'It is one of the most important things for me: maybe because I'm from Italy, I always need lots of light and sunshine to get into the right frame of mind when I sit down to design' Barbara says.

This need for sky and sunshine led her to dropping a small but seductive landscaped roof terrace into the middle of the top floor plan. This bold move brings sun into her largely north-facing, double-height living space below, augmented by the reflection obtained from the white walls.

'I always insist with my clients that they should use natural materials, as I love how they age, and I'm drawn to their warmth. Wood lends itself perfectly to the home – it is timeless, and it only gets better with use.' In this house, full of bespoke joinery meticulously detailed, many different types of veneer are to be seen, in different combinations. For the entrance hall coat cupboard, the artist Kate Blee was brought in to design a screen made from a mixture of some solid cherry and walnut poles, while others are inspired by Bauhaus colours. 'The house,' Barbara says, 'is a very personal collage of different influences, personal preferences, creative ideas and experiments… in some extraordinary way, the plants bring it all together into a cohesive whole.'

An eight-year old avocado grown by Barbara from a pip reaches for the sky in the double-height volume of the open plan living room. Throughout the house, the furniture is eclectic; in the seating area it comprises an orange Elan sofa by Jasper Morrison for Cappellini, in stark contrast with a black 19th century Biedermeier one, chrome Eileen Grey side tables and a Le Corbusier armchair. The rug belonged to Barbara's grandparents. Throughout the house, walls are painted Dulux Brilliant White.

'Plants break up the rigidity of the lines and panels; they tie everything together.'

The generous open plan living room includes a sizeable and well-defined dining area. The narrow table, regularly seating 12, is painted in a pale mint colour – Mizzle by Farrow and Ball, protected by a strong varnish that makes the surface particularly impermeable, obviating the need for a tablecloth. The chairs are Thonet replicas, still manufactured in the Czech Republic. The pendant lights are Edwardian originals. A leggy Ficus Lyrata straddles the division between dining and seating areas.

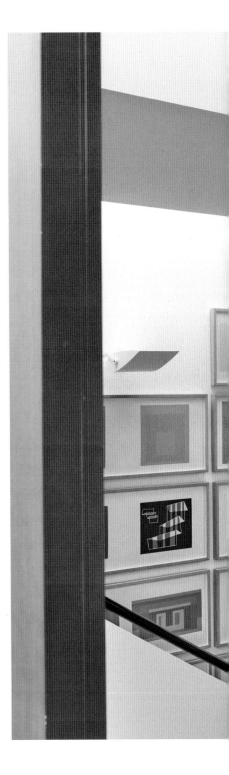

The bronze handrail to the main staircase – one of
Barbara's favourite details – is a direct quote from a similar
one at La Fondation Le Corbusier in Paris. The collection
of Josef Albers prints and the very healthy Papyra
Aquatica enhance the staircase leading to the terrace.

In the absence of a garden, a heavily planted roof terrace was inserted into the centre of the top floor. A southern-facing 'room without a roof', with brightly painted glazed red sliding doors, it provides an outdoor dining room while bringing year-round much daylight and sunlight into the living spaces below. The outdoor metal chairs are by Tolix, the table by Ikea. Many of the plants are herbs used daily in cooking.

Designed by the artist Kate Blee, a long-term friend of Barbara's, this sliding door to a coat cupboard was inspired by scaffolding seen by Kate in a recent trip to Uganda. The wooden poles are cherry and walnut.

On a hidden mezzanine high above the living area, a long bespoke walnut desk is flanked by a healthy Chinese money plant.

Antonino Sciortino

Sculptor
Milan, Italy

PLANTS DON'T TEND TO COME MORE super-sized than in the home of Antonino Sciortino. Giant succulents, cacti and agave overflow from enormous pots the size of armchairs, while olive trees shoot out of containers bigger than footstools. They are memories in physical form, all grown from cuttings taken in his native Sicily, evocative in their arid, Mediterranean beauty. 'I love them and I carefully take care of them,' he says. 'They remind me of my homeland. Their smells and their colours are the best and most authentic souvenirs of where I'm from.' As a connection to a home he can't get to very often, being around these plants puts him at ease. 'They make me feel well,' he says. 'But then, I've always been fascinated by the idea of living in a greenhouse.'

Antonino's home – or greenhouse, depending on how you look at it – is south-facing, with numerous windows: the ideal place to keep plants. 'After thriving through a bright winter, the plants go out into the garden in spring, returning invigorated in the autumn,' Antonino says, adding that keeping them on trolleys means he can move them around with ease. Having an exterior garden is a rarity for the city, especially in this cobbled neighbourhood. His local area has become the city's arts district in the time he has been living here, a luxury he takes full advantage of. 'I confess that, after lunch, I'll curl up on the sofa and fall asleep looking at the garden plants. These are details that give me tranquillity. A true treat for Milan.'

His apartment is arranged over two floors, and is now mostly open-plan. Space was needed for the large foliage, of course, but Antonino says: 'We created airy and liveable rooms with hardly any walls because we liked the idea of being able to communicate easily from one end to the other.' In his work, he creates mostly with iron, so it's perhaps no surprise that metal features prominently in his home. The long, delicate rods of the staircase run from the ground floor to the very top of the apartment, emphasising the height of the space, while many of the trollies on which the plants stand are iron, too. Blending the metal with concrete floors and whitewashed walls, Antonino's style leans towards industrial. 'I like the original colours of the materials,' he says. 'The iron is dark, the concrete is grey, the fabrics are rough or discoloured by time and they enhance the green of the plants.' The only strong note of colour is the bright enamel of the lava stone on the kitchen table – a nod, Antonio says, to the 'opulent and decadent aesthetic of Sicily'.

What Antonino has done is create an oasis of home away from home, filled with pieces that make urban life feel a little more like the island on which he grew up. 'Although located in the city centre, it is surprisingly calm here,' Antonino says. 'Immersed in nature, nothing but serenity prevails.'

'They are memories in physical form, all grown from cuttings taken in his native Sicily, evocative in their arid, Mediterranean beauty.'

Made from Sicilian lava stone, the table was created by a local craftsman. Antonino designed the little black table himself.

Peter Huelster

Attorney
Brooklyn, New York, USA

THE SHOW-STOPPING FEATURE OF Peter Huelster's family home has got to be the living wall. Over six metres (20 feet) tall, it snakes beguilingly up the double-height extension, the leaves of the ficus and fern fronds bristling gently in the breeze that wafts in when the powder-coated steel windows are cranked open. It has brought the back of the house quite literally to life,' Peter says. 'The kids have grown up playing with it, clipping butterflies they've made in craft classes to it, painting its leaves, even hiding in it.' He and his wife Allison, who runs an arts organisation, have to trim it regularly to stop it taking over, and gently mist it with water, but otherwise the ever-changing installation pretty much takes care of itself. 'I'm not sure if we appreciated how big it would get,' Peter says.

Created for the home by Kim Hoyt of Kim Hoyt Architecture/Landscape, the living wall's existence was always part of the plan for this city home in Fort Greene, an artsy neighbourhood of Brooklyn, New York. Peter and Allison liked the area for its proliferation of parks and green squares, but it was still imperative to forge as much of a link to the outside as they could, to disguise the fact they live in such an urban place. When they found the house, it was a crumbled wreck. 'It was in awful shape,' Peter says. 'There was so much water damage to the back of the building. We had to tread a fine line between a gut renovation and preservation of what was here. We wanted to respect the original build, but there was a lot that needed work.'

The couple enlisted the help of the architect Elizabeth Roberts, who came up with the brainwave of opening up the back of the house entirely with glass. 'The lower floor was very dark and cramped and depressing,' Peter says. 'And we couldn't figure out how to brighten it up. Elizabeth showed us how to embrace some of the building's original design, by keeping the ceilings low in the kitchen to create a feeling of cosiness, and then having these big windows at the back, which truly bring the outdoors in.' Creating an atrium at the rear of the home allowed for double fenestration: the living area upstairs has windows that open into the atrium, allowing natural light to flood in. 'We purposefully avoided anything too busy at this end, like a rear staircase, to really make the home feel bright,' Peter says.

Elsewhere, the project focused much more on enhancement than alteration. 'The beams were in great shape,' Peter says, of the timber that lines the kitchen ceiling. 'Leaving them exposed was a way to not only celebrate their beauty, but also allow a little more height in this already small space.' Marble and light wood worktops contrast with dark limestone flooring by Lapicida, all of which is brightened by those colossal windows. 'I'm so glad we chose foliage rather than more traditional art to line that wall,' Peter says. 'We'd have needed massive artworks if we wanted them not to be dwarfed in that space. Far better to let nature be the well-deserving star.'

Made up of ficus and fern plants, this installation designed by Kim Hoyt has become another member of the family. It provides a backdrop to family life, often being a place for the children to clip their art to.

'The living wall snakes beguilingly up the double-height extension, the leaves of the ficus and fern fronds bristling gently in the breeze.'

Swathed in reclaimed herringbone parquet, the stairs
are painted in Off Black by Farrow & Ball, creating
a dramatic entrance.

This is a low space, in contrast to the cavernous
atrium it sits next to. Rich colours were used in the
kitchen to keep it feeling cosy. The cabinets are by
Wood Mode, painted in Newport Green by Benjamin
Moore. The limestone flooring is by Lapicida.

Landscape architect Kim Hoyt turned the back of the house into an outdoor room, complete with Lapicida floor tiles, which flow into the dining area just inside the powder-coated steel doors.

Emma and Ross Perkin

Architects, and co-founders of Emil Eve Architects
Stoke Newington, London, UK

'WE'RE ALWAYS TRYING TO LISTEN to the building: to uncover what it was, work out what's important to keep and where we can change things to suit new uses and new people,' says architect Emma Perkin of the ethos she shares with her husband Ross. They co-founded Emil Eve Architects, a London-based agency that draws on his background as a conservation architect and their shared love of colour, materials and textures. Their aim is to lovingly and respectfully blur the line between period buildings and contemporary ideas.

Nowhere is this better demonstrated than in their own home. A plant-filled, carefully renovated Victorian end-of-terrace house in Stoke Newington, London, its staircase is a shining example of the Emil Eve touch. On the lower run, leading up from the open-plan kitchen-diner extension, a blue Valchromat balustrade rises sharply, meeting the original banisters on the turn. 'We wanted to mark the difference between new and old,' Emma says. 'The two diagonals weave together like layers, telling the story of the house.'

Next to the staircase, telling its own story, a four metre (13 foot) plant climbs between the floors. 'Ross bought it about two years ago, and it must be so happy in that spot,' Emma says. 'A case of right plant, right place. You can almost see it growing.' Curiously, for someone so meticulous about everything that has gone into her home that she knows the name of the bricks used in the extension (Petersen Tegl, chosen because they complement both the oak inside and the aged Victorian brick of the main house), Emma doesn't know what type of plant it is. 'I never know the names,' Emma says. 'Though I just couldn't live without them.' About 80 per cent of the plants in her home are cuttings from her mother's plants, or from those of their friends, and are chosen and positioned in order to perform different functions. In the bathroom, smaller, darker plants are placed to pick out the dark tones of the tiles and create a calming space, while in the main bedroom, there are lighter, more uplifting plants. In the extension, plants help to bring the verdant outdoors in, framing the picture window and creating a connection with the courtyard. 'You can see them as you walk in the front door, and it links the feeling of greenery all the way through the house,' Emma says.

Emma and Ross are particularly interested in joinery, and designed the kitchen, dining table and sliding doors to the outside themselves. The windows flow around two sides of the home, and finding doors that didn't have beams in the middle was impossible, so the couple had to create a system bespoke. The concrete floor is, Emma says, a really 'basic concrete concrete mix, but instead of simply polishing it, which has become the norm, we decided grind it back further bringing out the material's texture like a terrazzo. We love it! Not only is it the most forgiving floor in the world – our children can happily drop cereal on it – it was another chance for us to work with a simple material and find a way to elevate it.' Texture is always important, and exposed oak was used purposefully: 'We use timbers like paint colours, and oak had the natural warmth we were after for this space.' Oiling rather than applying a varnish to the surface of the timber stemmed from a desire to appreciate its raw beauty. 'It's a family home,' Emma says, 'and you have to accept it will age and mark. But again, those scratches tell the story of our life here, and so we enjoy the process of aging gracefully.' An ethos that truly accepts that a house should also be a home.

Through the giant sliding doors, the courtyard is wrapped in Petersen Tegl bricks, which pick up the tones of the oak used inside. 'They are all handmade, with slightly wobbly surfaces, so they also complement the aged Victorian brick on the original part of the house,' Emma says.

'Their aim is to lovingly and respectfully blur the line between period buildings and contemporary ideas.'

In the open-plan extension, Emma and Ross designed the oak dining table and bookcases themselves. The chairs are vintage, concrete floor was ground back to truly enjoy the texture of the aggregate within. The pendant light is by Viabizzuno.

Contemporary design meets period detail as the Valchromat lower level intersects with the original bannister. The creeping plant, whose name Emma doesn't know, is over four metres (13 feet) tall.

Ross designed the kitchen, and the island is made in Valchromat. Its surface is oak, to match the table and bookcases that line the wall, and it is illuminated by lights from Tala. The tiles behind the sink are from Grestec. Chinese money plants, monsteras plants and spider plants line the shelf above them.

Here, the dark green plants were kept small, as Emma thinks this helps to create a cocooning, enclosed, relaxing feel. They were chosen to complement the dark green tiles from Johnson Tiles. The floor tiles are from Mink Interiors.

In the living area, pots and plants line the mantle. 'I don't think of myself as a collector,' Emma says. 'I think we just accumulate things we like.' A lot of the pots were picked up from local makers on trips to Scottish islands. 'They're all different, but reflect the culture of each place.'

With walls painted in Paint & Paper Library's Slate I, the plants here are purposefully lighter, chosen to feel both calming and uplifting.

John Sinclair and Alice Saunders

Co-founder of design agency ustwo and rug designer,
Kent, UK

'I LOVE OLD THINGS: I LIKE BRINGING them back to life. Nurturing them. Plants are the same. I like the idea you can put care into them and they'll grow and develop,' says John Sinclair, co-founder of design company ustwo. The home he shares with his partner, the rug designer Alice Saunders, is testament to their shared passion for restoring and repairing. A once dilapidated barn, it has been turned into an architectural wonder, complete with a helter-skelter staircase and clever window tricks (more on those later).

It has become, John says, 'a pet rescue centre for plants. Anything that is too big or too weird, I'll end up taking in and giving a home.' He's referring to the two giant fig trees that the London restaurant Chiltern Firehouse had once paid £2,000 ($2,700) for, but which had since grown a little scrappy. Being too tall for most homes, they were delighted when the couple offered to have them. However, the barn itself could have been deemed 'too big and weird' by many. Now, as Alice says, 'all the textures and the plant life make it feel very calming,' but that wasn't always the case. Set in the North Downs of Kent, south-east England, surrounded by fields and not too far from the coast, it was in a sorry state when John bought it in 2011. 'In fact, it was falling apart,' John says. 'The weatherboards had gone, the floor was just mud. It would have been cheaper to knock it down. But instead I decided to build around it, out of respect for the original stuff.'

The process was tricky. First, planning restraints meant they couldn't add any more windows than had been in the original structure, which wouldn't have been enough to create a habitable living space. The solution came from an inspired idea: the windows at the end of the lounge area are actually internal, part of a wall built just inside the barn's big doors.

Keeping the doors open lets the light in. Then they had to work out a way to heat the open-plan, 300-square-metre (980-square-foot) home. 'The whole look of the space was a result of a series of decisions based around heating,' John says. 'There is no gas in this area, so we decided on ground source, and the house needed to be insulated as well as it could be. With high ceilings, wall-mounted radiators send the heat up the side, so the only way to be efficient in a very tall space is to have the heating flat across the ground. So then concrete was the obvious choice for underfloor heating. Then I had to use a lot of wood to soften the concrete, and plants to make the industrial structure seem homely.' As a result, foliage is everywhere: hanging over the mezzanine, shooting up out of the pots on ledges. 'And the word "homely" is the first one people use when they come over,' Alice says.

Aside from the plants, it's the flooring – huge beams reclaimed from an old bridge – and the staircase that steal the show. 'That's the money shot,' John says. 'It's mega clever, because it not only supports the mezzanine, but also the chimney and open fire.' It wasn't without its challenges: the way the chimney tapers means the staircase gets wider the higher up you go, but planning demands stairs are all the same width for safety. 'Or at least, that they appear the same width,' John says. 'We painted the edges of each tread black, more so at the top, tricking the eye. The planners loved it!'

There are plans for the couple to increase the storage, something John admits he should have considered more when he built it, but in the meantime, the indoor garden grows. 'My summer job as a teenager was a gardener,' John says. 'I've always loved being around plants. What you put into them, you get back.'

Under the mezzanine level sits a Chesterfield sofa John bought 20 years ago, and an Eames Lounge Chair. The beams that line the ceiling above are from the original barn, and instead of covering them up, John chose to make a feature of them, to be true to the building's origins. The flooring is made from huge planks taken from a decommissioned bridge John bought online, which initially seemed like a bargain, but actually cost more to restore than he could have imagined.

Open-plan to the kitchen, the lengthy dining table was made from an old ten-pin bowling lane John bought online. 'It's maple, and built to withstand heavy balls being chucked at it, so it's hard as nails and ideal for a table,' John says. The chairs are from the Scandinavian auction house Borkowski, and are dwarfed by the Philodendron Xanadu in the window. The kitchen stools were bought after John spotted them in London restaurant Tonkotsu, where they had been made by a member of staff, and the island worktop is fashioned from mahogany boards that were previously used for clay to cool on after leaving the kiln.

'I've always loved being around plants. What you put into them, you get back.'

The bath is from Lefroy Brooks, and sits under hanging spider plants.

On the ground floor, the bedroom is in one of the barn's old stable blocks. There is more concrete flooring here, and a large Dracaena trifasciata, or mother-in-law's tongue, in a steel canister.

About the Authors

Jennifer Haslam

Jennifer Haslam is a UK-based Interiors Stylist and Creative Consultant. Passionate about creating beautiful compositions to produce striking imagery, she has spent the last 15 years working with global brands, international publishers as well as smaller start ups. With a keen interest in architecture and the way people live with design, her work has been featured in *ELLE Decoration*, *Livingetc*, and the *Sunday Times* to name a few. After many years living in London, she now lives in York with her husband Strider, two boys Arlo and Vinny, Sprollie dog Pip, and a small jungle of houseplants.

Pip McCormac

Having been an interiors and lifestyle journalist for almost 20 years, Pip is now the editor of *Livingetc*, the UK's leading contemporary design brand. He has previously worked at *ELLE Decoration*, *Red*, *Sunday Times Style* and *Grazia*, and written for publications such as *The Guardian*, *ES Magazine* and *Stylist*. He recently relocated from London to Somerset, where he lives with several Monstera, cacti and a philodendron. This is his fourth book.

Acknowledgments

Pip McCormac

A huge thanks has to go out to every homeowner who agreed to take part in this book. My conversations with them have been fascinating, eye-opening and given me a new perspective on design.

Thanks to Daniel New, whose work on the design of the pages has helped bring the words and pictures to life, and to Eve Marleau for commissioning this dream project and giving us such fantastic encouragement and space to shape it how we liked.

Simon Bevan, I'm so grateful for all the work that went into the taking of the images - you've captured the essence of each home perfectly.

And Jennifer Haslam – you're amazing! Thank you for tirelessly keeping this project on track, updating the doc, giving us focus and turning in a continuous stream of stellar photos. I genuinely couldn't have done this without you. Thank you!

Jennifer Haslam

Firstly the hugest of thanks to the team at Hardie Grant, in particular Eve Marleau for all her expertise, excitement and guidance and, for giving us the opportunity to create this book.

My lovely Co-Author Pip McCormac, it has been a complete joy to work on with you from start to finish. Your words are magical and bring such beauty and knowledge to the pages, it's been a dream project.

A heartfelt thanks to Simon Bevan for his stunning photography, wonderful creativity through the lens, and great humour on set, it's been such a beautiful project to shoot with you, I truly thank-you. We also couldn't have done it without the help of Ian Tillotson, and Laura Falconer, I'm so pleased you were both able to share and work on this with us,

And, of course a big thanks to the international photographers, who have stepped in for us when travel was not possible, Niki Sebastian, Marnie Hawson, Nathalie Artaxo, Matthew Williams, Lars house, Brooklyn, etc (can I cross check the full list of names of people we have images from)

To Daniel New who has created the most beautifully designed pages, and has embraced and shared our vision for the project.

To all the homeowners who have kindly opened their doors to us, it's been wonderful meeting everyone of you, and truly inspiring to share your homes with you. To all the architects, designers and people who have helped along the way in the introductions and leads of finding the homes too.

And finally, a very special thank-you to my family, my husband Strider, who is unbelievably understanding, patient and just says yes when I announce I have to "work again". My two little boys, who have coped amazingly when I've been shooting away, and lastly to my parents, who have always supported me, and told me to 'just go for it', I'll forever be grateful for your encouragement.

Published in 2021 by Hardie Grant Books,
an imprint of Hardie Grant Publishing

Hardie Grant Books (London)
5th & 6th Floors
52–54 Southwark Street
London SE1 1UN

Hardie Grant Books (Melbourne)
Building 1, 658 Church Street
Richmond, Victoria 3121

hardiegrantbooks.com

British Library Cataloguing-in-Publication Data. A catalogue record for this
book is available from the British Library.

A New Leaf
ISBN: 978-1-78488-462-8

10 9 8 7 6 5 4 3 2 1

Publisher: Kajal Mistry
Commissioning Editor: Eve Marleau
Design: Daniel New
Photographers: Simon Bevan, Nicki Sebastian, Nathalie Artaxo for
Historias de Casa, Marnie Hawson, Bruce Damonte, Grant Harder,
Serge Anton, Matthew Williams, Dustin Acksland
Art Director and Stylist: Jennifer Haslam
Copy-editor: Tara O'Sullivan
Production Controller: Katie Jarvis

Colour reproduction by p2d
Printed and bound in China by Leo Paper Products Ltd.

Artwork Credits

Valentina Audrito
P42 – artist unknown

Brigette Romanek
P46 – artist unknown
P50 – artist unknown
P51 – artist unknown
P55 – artist unknown
P57 – artist unknown

Nick Douwma and Kara Melchers
P60 – *Cronos*, Stanley William Hayter
P62 – *Putting the pieces together II*, Kim Bartelt
P64 – *Sequence 01*, Formworks
P65 – *Etching Outside the Studio*, Leigh Bird, *Nude in Red*, Alexandria Coe
P66 – *Owl*, Tracey Emin

Fi Lindsay
P88 – title unknown, Ian Chamberlain, Rabley Gallery
P91 – title unknown, Emma Stibley, Rabley Gallery
P95 – title unknown, Kitty Sterling
P96 – title unknown, Katherine Jones, Rabley Gallery

Adrian and Megan Corrigall
P116 – *Boy with Kite*, Hugh Aylett
P120 – *Work Hard and be Nice to People*, Anthony Burrill
P118 – titles unknown, Sean Pollock. Title unknown, Ray Smith

Robert Storey
P132 – *Handsome Yellow Caterpillar*, Andrej Dúbravský, 2019
P134 – *The Red Sky on the After Party*, Andrej Dúbravský, 2020
P136 – *Playground*, John Booth, 2017

Millie and Dave Wells
P150 – title unknown, Willy Nakanbala Tjungarrayi, Papunya Tjupi Arts

Lars Richardson
P174 – artist unknown
P183 – artist unknown

Barbara Weiss
P192 – artist unknown, Josef Albers

Antonino Sciortino
P198 – artist unknown
P204 – artists unknown

Peter Huelster
P216 – *Cine Campoamor*, Andrew Moore, from the *Cuba* series
P217 – *Victoria with Cat*, Alice Neel, 1981
P221 – *Central Park Bandshell*, William Kentridge, 2005

Emma and Ross Perkin
P226 – title unknown, David Nash
P228 – title unknown, Nigel Peake, title unknown, Ian Angus, title unknown,
Gerald McKnight (Emma's grandfather)
P237 – title unknown, Sally Graham (Emma's mother), title unknown,
Gerald McKnight

John Sinclair and Alice Saunders
P251 – artist unknown

*Every reasonable effort has been made to acknowledge the copyright
of artworks in this volume. Any errors or omissions that may have
occurred are inadvertent, and will be corrected in subsequent
editions provided notification is sent in writing to the publisher.*